Fast Acting, Long Lasting

MANIS FRIEDMAN

Fast Acting, Long Lasting

What You Need to Know
for Successful Dating

IT'S GOOD TO KNOW PUBLISHING
New York

Copyright © 2023 Manis Friedman. All rights reserved.
Printed in the United States of America. No part of this book may be used, reproduced, translated, electronically stored, or transmitted in any manner whatsoever without prior written permission from the publisher, except by reviewers, who may quote brief passages in their reviews.

For information, contact:
It's Good to Know Publishing
Brooklyn, New York
ItsGoodToKnowPublishing.com
Email: info@itsgoodtoknowpublishing.com

Library of Congress Control Number: 2022901311

ISBN: 979-8-9854477-4-3 (trade paperback)
ISBN: 979-8-9854477-5-0 (ebook)

10 9 8 7 6 5 4 3 2 1

Note to the reader: The stories and examples in this book reflect the issues and questions that have recurred during many years of Rabbi Manis Friedman's public classes and private counseling sessions. However, the characters described and the details of their lives are composites, and resemblance to any particular person or event is purely accidental and unintentional. Names and details have been changed.

The information and insights in this book are solely the opinion of the author and should not be considered as a form of therapy, advice, direction, diagnosis, and/or treatment of any kind. This information is not a substitute for medical, psychological, or other professional advice, counseling, or care. All matters pertaining to your individual health should be supervised by a physician or appropriate health-care practitioner. Neither the publisher nor the author assume any responsibility or liability whatsoever on behalf of any purchaser or reader.

Cover design and interior layout by Kanner.co

CONTENTS

	Introduction:	
	The Future Is Not What It Used to Be	vii
1	Marriage Readiness 101	1
2	Picture the Life You Want to Live	7
3	The Magic List	13
4	No Need to Worry	17
5	Why You Can't Lose Your Soulmate	21
6	The Question That Changes Everything	25
7	What Is "Good Chemistry"?	29
8	The Key to Safe, Sane, and Constructive Dating	31
9	Toxic Idea: Maybe I'll Never Get Married	35
10	Shidduch Crisis: Myth or Fact?	37
11	Does the Shadchan System Still Work?	39
12	The Art of Optimism	43
13	What Will My Friends Think?	47
14	Am I Being Too Picky?	51
15	How to Prevent Dating Suicide	53
16	The Golden Rule in Dating	57
17	Is This It? How to Know If She's the One	61
18	The Secret to Praying for Your Shidduch	63
19	Fast Track to Your Bashert?	65
20	Bonus: The Three-Word Marriage Guidebook	69
	Acknowledgments	71

INTRODUCTION

The Future Is Not What It Used to Be

The prognosis has changed concerning almost every aspect of social life, but most glaringly in the dating process.

For many decades the prediction was that relationships between men and women will become more liberal, more permissive, and more experimental. It was believed that this would result in healthier, stronger, long-lasting marriages. That belief is gone.

The future cannot be what it used to be because all the experts agree that the vast social experiment of the 60s and 70s has proven to be a failure. Dating as it is known today is, for all practical purposes, a trial marriage or an alternative to marriage, or even simply playing house.

The prospects of healthy marriage are being lost. Back in the 40s, my father-in-law, Rabbi Sholom Ber Gordon, OBM, was a teenager in New York. He reported to the draft board of the United States Army for his mandatory physical. The Army psychiatrist (who happened to be Jewish), seeing a young man with a full beard, said to him in Yiddish, "Vos tust du da? (What are you doing here?) You don't belong here."

He then asked him a series of questions: Do you have a girlfriend? Do you go to movies? Do you date girls?

To all these questions the answer was no.

"But you do intend to get married?" the intrigued psychiatrist asked.

To which he said, "Yes." The psychiatrist frowned and classified Rabbi Gordon as "mentally unstable but nonviolent" and sent him home.

That's what the future used to be. Today, the more traditional dating rules are becoming popular. The prognosis now is people will be getting married the good old-fashioned way.

It would be ironic if at the same time that the world as a whole is catching on to what tradition has always offered, the frum community is stuck experimenting with the very behavior that others are now abandoning.

It is therefore necessary to review "the rules of engagement," to appreciate the wisdom, the elegance, and the thoughtfulness of the Jewish way of dating, which has proven to be both fast acting and long lasting.

Although this book does contain some basic rules, it is primarily a hashkafa on the principles of marriage and the best way to get there.

You may already know much of the advice in this book but may not appreciate how crucial and helpful this knowledge is and what a tremendous difference it makes to your marriage, your family, your children, and the community at large.

The future is not what it used to be—it's looking much better.

Hatzlacha on your dating and let us know of your success.

Rabbi Manis Friedman

> "Matchmaker, Matchmaker,
> Make me a match."
>
> —*Fiddler on the Roof*

CHAPTER ONE

Marriage Readiness 101

Am I ready for marriage? How will I ever know that I am ready to be married?

Marriage is a transformative act of the first order. Without question, there is no other step you could take that will so fundamentally alter the course of your life. Not a career choice, not a relocation, perhaps not even having a child, will so color all subsequently chosen paths as the person you will marry and the kind of marriage you build with him or her. It is no wonder, then, that a person could be paralyzed by the question: *Am I ready for this?*

As timely as the question is, the truth is that asking it accomplishes little. Its principal function is as a form of self-torture. This is because the answer is that you may never *feel* ready. Perversely, if you get to the point where you finally think you are ready for marriage, it is probably an indication of how *unready* you really are. Marriage is an endlessly challenging, lofty, and all-consuming engagement. There is no way one could declare oneself "ready" for it without sounding, if not foolish, then at least brazen. How could one understand ahead of time all that is involved?

So you are probably not going to feel ready. Therefore, we don't wait for a sign, or a moment, or an epiphany before deciding to get married, because none of those things are likely to happen. Instead, eventually, circumstances align, the right people are present, and it is the time to get married, so we get married. Ready or not.

Still, you want a sign. If you could discern some signal in yourself that you are ready for marriage, what might it be?

The one truly decisive indication that you are in the right frame of mind for the momentous undertaking of marriage is the recognition that you are open to having another person in your life.

It took such a long while for you to learn how to grow up. For so long your parents did your laundry, kept the house warm for you, fed you, and made sure you were polite to the neighbors. But at a certain point, the custodial care waned. Even if a child still lives at home while he or she goes to college or works at a job, the relationship with one's parents has shifted. Bank accounts, buying their first car, and learning to build healthy relationships with peers are no longer under parental supervision. If a child has been raised well, this transition is fairly smooth and often exhilarating. However, as natural and healthy as it is to learn to stand on your own feet, it is nevertheless not the endgame. For we are not meant to go through life alone, "free" and unaccountable to anyone. Remember: it's not good to be alone.

Hopefully, we were not alone during our childhood. The familial relationships of our young years are part of our earliest cognizance. Even when the family dance is irritating, or even infuriating, it is a familiar dance. We know what to expect from our parents and siblings. We are comforted by that familiarity.

Marriage is wholly different. In marriage, one basically links one's life and fate to a stranger. It is not comfortable at all. It is, however, as exhilarating as one can get in life. Apparently, that is what G-d wants for us—both the discomfort and the exhilaration—for in the Torah it says that a man will leave his father and his mother and cleave to his wife. Totally normal, the way of the world, this business of becoming one with a stranger and building a life with him. But let's be honest: this is going to be a big deal. The amount of kindness, generosity, and tolerance needed to share a life seems so immense that it feels like it is beyond the capability of a human being. Can anyone ever really be capable enough for this? Who among us is really that good?

So if you are questioning your *capability*, then you are being rational, for can one ever be completely ready to share his or her life with another person? Yet, despite the rational hesitations, we get married anyway. We don't do it because we think we are saints and therefore capable of all that goodness. No, we know we aren't perfect and still we get married. Why? Aren't we likely to fail?

The same question could be asked about anything else we do in Judaism. One could easily ask a Jew, "You're going to 'serve' G-d? Study His Torah? Pray? Fulfill His commandments? You have the audacity, the temerity, and the boldness to presume that you know how to serve the Creator, know what He wants, and communicate with Him? What a presumption!"

Of course, we don't really presume to be so knowledgeable or insightful, but what does that have to do with it? G-d told us to study and pray and fulfill commandments so we do these things. Are we "good at it"? We don't even think this way. If we did, we would be so intimidated by the scale of the task that we wouldn't be able to take action. On the other hand, if we ever did delude ourselves into thinking that we were worthy enough to properly serve G-d, then we would have to start all over again, because it's not right to serve G-d with such a lack of humility and self-awareness.

In this same way, we approach marriage. Marriage isn't something you get "good" at. Marriage is a mitzvah. It's holiness. It's an affair of the soul, which means it's not something to be taken lightly. It's not like picking up a new hobby or a sport, nor is it a game. Marriage is as serious as life itself, and we're not expected to ever get "good" at marriage just as we're not expected to be "good" at life.

If you are the parent of a child who claims she is not yet ready for marriage, yet in your own assessment she is a mature and capable woman, what can you do to get her to move forward? In such a case, you are going to have to wait patiently until your daughter feels she is ready. If she is *actually* immature and incapable but tells you she is ready to get married, then you have a problem. But if she is truly mature and capable, then trust her and let her find her way. She will find her bashert.

Do we know what we're doing before we get married? Of course not! Do we think we are going to be super good at marriage? Not the point. We don't know what we're doing, and we have no idea how "good" we will be at it. But as with all other G-dly endeavors, we do what we're told, and we do our best. That's all anyone can do.

Marriage is as serious as
life itself, and we're not expected to
ever get "good" at marriage just as we're
not expected to be "good" at life.

CHAPTER TWO

Picture the Life You Want to Live

Everyone waits for vacation time; it is a welcome break from work and an exciting change from daily life. Imagine if a person arrived at the airport on the first day of his vacation without a clue about his destination. Or imagine that he had an idea of where he wanted to go, but before the vacation started he hadn't made a single hotel reservation or checked out any interesting attractions at the destination.

That doesn't bode well for a successful holiday. He will waste precious time on disappointing side trips, wrong turns, and unsatisfactory arrangements. Without a doubt, the essential key to a great vacation is prior planning, and without a clear vision of the destination, such planning is impossible.

What about marriage? Where do you want to end up in marriage? What is your desired destination? What is your vision of marriage?

Try imagining yourself ten years into your hypothetical marriage. What do you look like? Are you sitting on a beach somewhere, eyeing the world through very expensive sunglasses? Do you see yourself wandering through a mansion filled with fancy furniture? What does your family look like? Are you a multitasking dynamo juggling work and family schedules? Or, maybe you picture yourself sitting on a couch with six kids climbing all over you, three of them in diapers. Is one of these you?

What about the spirit and atmosphere of your home? Do you envision a Shabbat table full of guests and a husband who inspires everyone with his brilliance? Perhaps you picture a Shabbat table full of guests who are being inspired by *your* brilliance. How are your children dressed for Shabbat? What about your home is going to inspire you and your family and your guests?

Here is a useful exercise: take a pen and try to articulate on paper what it is that people will be inspired by in your home. This is an essential component of envisioning your future.

Our lives are not only, and not even mainly, about the jobs we are busy with and the errands we are checking off our lists. We are carried through the vicissitudes of our jobs and our daily hiccups by our faith and the ideals that inspire us.

We learn inspiration from the lives we see others living; we carry it away and try to incorporate it into our own lives. Sometimes the inspiration is positive, sometimes what we see is decidedly negative, in which case the example is an instructive cautionary lesson.

Projecting ahead as part of your vision of the future, what impression will your home leave on others?

All of this is an important first step. It's very simple: if you know what you want your life to be, then you can figure out what you need to do to get there. Once you know where you want to go, you can find someone headed in the same direction and arrive at the same destination together.

Sometimes it happens that a person who has been dating for years without success will ask me why she still hasn't found someone to marry. When I ask her, "What do you want out of life? Where do you picture yourself in the future?" it often turns out that the kind of life she wants to live is not one that is compatible with marriage. If this is true of you, that you desire to get married but marriage doesn't fit in with the picture you envision for your life, you're setting yourself up for failure. If marriage won't get you to the place that you want to be, then you're going to have a tough time getting and staying married.

Even if you see marriage as a centerpiece of your future life, it is helpful to understand yourself well enough to manage your expectations. If you were one of those people imagining herself in the mansion with all the fancy furnishings, then you shouldn't marry a man who teaches in cheder or in a yeshiva. They don't go together! Or if it is truly important to you to marry someone working in Jewish outreach or education, then the sooner you come to grips with your desire for riches, the better.

Sometimes the problem is that a person isn't quite sure where he wants to go. He hasn't figured out his own life and in which direction he wants to head. This is also a problem, for marriage means that you are ready to share your life with another person. If you have no idea what your life is all about, then what are you sharing? Being ready for marriage means that one has a vision of a life he would like to build, and the realization that it would be a lot more fun to accomplish it with someone else than to do it by himself.

Over and over people underestimate the importance of this very practical notion. The hoped-for romantic story arc goes like this: A person meets someone with whom he falls in love, the feeling is reciprocated, then the two lovebirds marry and they spend their lives loving each other to pieces. While this may sound blissful, it's not actually a plan for the future. It's not a strategy, it's just hope.

This classic romantic view of marriage has vaulted love (of the initial exciting type) into a position it doesn't deserve—as if it is the key to the success of a marriage. People say, "As long as they love each other, then..." Then what? Then everything will turn out great? Clearly, this is not true. The truth is that marriage is not all about love, or rather, not *only* about love. In fact, it is served much better by compassion and respect. Mostly, marriage is about building a life together. This is why we bless a new husband and wife at their wedding that they should merit to build a *binyan adei ad*, an everlasting edifice. To build an everlasting edifice one needs a plan and a partner who shares that vision.

Marriage is a project, a plan that is larger than the two of you. So rather than making the mistake of thinking that it's all about me loving you and you loving me, understand that it is really about both of us loving marriage.

What you write on your paper is crucial: sketching out your future and developing a vision for your life removes much of the guesswork from looking for a spouse. If you have never before imagined what your future will look like, then now is the time to start.

Spend less time thinking about what kind of spouse you want and more time thinking about what kind of spouse you're going to be.

CHAPTER THREE

The Magic List

By this time we have all become conditioned to the online shopping experience. Type "curtains" in the search bar of your favorite device. You will be offered an array of filters: length, color, fabric, style, price. In the end, you choose between the last few options still standing. It is such a rational process that perhaps it's natural to assume we can use a similar process to choose a spouse.

It doesn't really work like that. The truth is that long before you started looking for your spouse, G-d had already hand-picked him or her. Even before you were born, G-d had decided whom you would eventually marry. Somewhere in the world, your spouse is hanging around waiting for you to find him. In fact, he's probably looking for you. Furthermore, by this point in your lives, both of you have already traveled a great distance to come into contact with one another. You are close to finding one another. The process of dating is the process of finding *him*. It is not a process of choosing the most desirable man or woman off the shelf. You are only trying to find your spouse; all the other singles on the shelf are irrelevant to this search. There really is nothing to be done about it now. He or she is ready; they already traveled quite a distance to get to you.

Does making a list of qualities that you are looking for in a spouse make sense in this scenario? Is this an attempt to apply some sort of filtering system to the search for your spouse?

One of the most beneficial byproducts of this whole process is what one gains in self-understanding. Making a list of what is important to you in a spouse is a function of gaining clarity. You are coming to a clearer understanding of yourself, a great step in finding your spouse. If you know what's going on in your own mind, you will be able to breathe more easily while dating. So go ahead and make a list.

When it comes to meeting a prospective suitor, don't take that list too seriously. Whatever list you might have made about what was important to you is not going to change whomever it is G-d decreed you will marry. You may be in for a surprise; eventually, you might discover that your intended doesn't fit all those criteria. He might not have the beard you imagined your husband would have. Or be as funny. Or as brilliant. He might be planning to be a plumber instead of a lawyer. (He will still make a good living!) Know a couple where the wife is a head taller than her husband? Do you think they planned it that way? Surely not, and yet they seem to be happily married.

Of course, there are essential elements that you are looking for in your husband or wife, and if you do not see them in the person you are dating, then he is not your husband. The crucial point is that these essential elements are factors that you have come to after serious introspection. For instance, you may know about yourself that you have a tendency to get overexcited about most things, and you understand that you must marry a calm, placid person. And conversely, you will bring excitement into the life of this calm person. Another example: you may know about yourself that you are easily stressed and therefore marrying someone who comes from a completely unfamiliar cultural background is going to add too many stress points in your life. You are looking for your husband to come from a similar background to your own. These factors are not arbitrary, they demonstrate a true understanding of yourself, an understanding of you that G-d, by the way, shares.

If a person could custom design his or her spouse, he or she would probably end up marrying something akin to a robot. Perfect features, a flawless operating system, answering all needs on demand. No flaws, yes, but also no soul. Thankfully, G-d had your soul in mind and has done the choosing, so you don't have to worry.

Rather than spending a whole lot of time thinking about whom you are going to marry, it is much more productive to think about how you are going to treat the one that you do marry. The best list you could make is a list of your goals about what you want to bring to a marriage. Spend less time thinking about what kind of spouse you want and more time thinking about what kind of spouse you're going to be.

CHAPTER FOUR

No Need to Worry

A lot of people worry about divorce. Even before they've met their spouse they are worried about divorce. Of course, it's perfectly natural when beginning a new project to worry about the prospect of failure. One thinks, *What if I make a mistake?* The more important the project, the more likely it is that this thought occurs.

Seeing other couples divorcing is discouraging and often leads to a misconception. Instead of wondering about the marriage and what might have been amiss in the married life of the couple, some singles think, *What if I marry the wrong person? What if I don't notice something ahead of time that I should have noticed?*

Divorce is no proof a mistake has been made or that the two people shouldn't have married. As a matter of fact, there is no such thing as the wrong two people getting married. That's an impossibility. (Remember Who did the choosing?) As long as the marriage took place, then the marriage was meant to happen.

So what did go wrong? It is possible that a person could be mistaken in their thinking about marriage. One may have married a person for the wrong reasons. In other words, it's the right husband, but she has the wrong expectations about what marriage is. Or it's the right wife, but he misled her with false pretenses and wrong information. If there were these mistakes of judgment or perception, there may eventually be a divorce.

Thinking that a marriage that ends in a divorce must have been a mistaken marriage is to completely undermine marriage itself. Divorce happens between two people who were meant to get married. The marriage proved to be too challenging or too painful, and in such a case, G-d gives a person a way to get out: divorce. But once again, that doesn't mean the marriage was a mistake. Both the marriage and the subsequent divorce were necessary situations that both people were meant to undergo.

Of course, ahead of time, you need to check carefully that this man or woman is the type of person with whom you want to build your life. If you have become engaged to someone you thought was going to be your wife, but you realize before getting married that you made a mistake in your thinking or judgment, simply adjust to reality, apologize for being wrong, and get on with your life.

In the same vein, young people whose parents modeled an unhappy or unsuccessful marriage may be burdened with the worry that they are doomed for lack of good role models in their youth. There are two ways to go with this history. One can always try to avoid the pain of examining one's past and end up not understanding it very well, in which case it's quite possible the patterns of the past will be repeated. The other possibility is to be enlightened. If you know that what you have seen and experienced as a child is something you don't want to repeat in your own marriage, you have a head start.

Of course, there is no guarantee that you will not repeat these mistakes. Hopefully, though, being aware of their consequences will keep you attuned to keep working on them. We are speaking here about the correct mindset to pursue marriage and not about how to raise children, which is a huge topic for another discussion. But for now, keep in mind that if you do repeat the mistakes of your parents, you will have children just like you! Your parents made those mistakes, and you are the result. Is that so bad?

The fact that there are no mistaken marriages should be very reassuring. It means you don't need to worry about marrying the wrong person, because there's no such thing.

You will marry the right person. Instead, sound, mature, and responsible thinking will lead you to ask, "Will I do the right thing once I'm married to the right person?"

CHAPTER FIVE

Why You Can't Lose Your Soulmate

Often we find a person who has trod a bumpy road before arriving at that point where he or she begins to look for a spouse. That road may have involved some unfortunate twists and turns.

I am frequently confronted by people like this who have fallen prey to the fearful notion that somehow their misbehavior may have jeopardized their chances to find and marry their intended mate. They fear that even though there is an intended soulmate for them, by a grievous error they have lost the chance to actually marry that person. The basic question is whether it is indeed possible to lose one's bashert, or, stated another way, that the soul originally meant for the person has slipped away.

This notion is entirely misbegotten. The Torah teaches us that every match is made in Heaven. We marry the one whom G-d has chosen for us to marry. If that is the case, then can one *lose* this soulmate? The answer is a simple *no*, you *cannot* lose your soulmate. The one whom G-d decreed you will marry *is* the one you will marry. Bashert means that it is meant to be. Saying that something is meant to be and that it also might not happen is logically contradictory and it is a foolish idea with which to torment oneself.

In this vein, there is another confusing idea making the rounds—that a person may have up to seven possible soulmates. Obviously, the worry for the anxious is *whether the one I am thinking of marrying is the one (out of seven) I really want to marry, or should I hang on and try to find another one of the seven?* Whether it's true that there really are seven possible soulmates is totally irrelevant to the process of finding your soulmate. It doesn't really matter how many possible matches there are; only one of them is going to be your spouse. You're going to end up with your spouse, and that's going to be the right one. The other possibilities were not the right one.

As we mentioned in the previous chapter, some people get married more than once. The fact that they do so doesn't mean they married "the wrong person." They married the right person but the marriage didn't work out—for any number of reasons. There are even some people who are destined to be married several times, but each marriage—even if it ended in divorce—was divinely ordained.

Let's take note that we don't apply this kind of thinking to other relationships. Can you imagine a parent looking at her child and declaring, "Whose kid is this? This is the wrong kid! You gave me the wrong child!" It wouldn't happen. Everyone knows the child you got is the right child, your child, the one meant for you to nurture and raise. In the same way, the spouse you marry is the right spouse. You won't end up with the wrong one.

Speculation about whether you have already missed out on marrying your soulmate is one worry you can shed. You *will* find your soulmate. It's just a matter of time.

Everyone knows the child you got
is the right child, your child, the one meant
for you to nurture and raise. In the same way,
the spouse you marry is the right spouse.
You won't end up with the wrong one.

CHAPTER SIX

The Question That Changes Everything

In the old days, the following scenario was quite common. A couple had a son and knew another couple with a daughter. While they were still children, the son and daughter were chosen for one another by their parents, who promised each other that they would marry the children to one another when the right time arrived. Eventually, the marriage took place, usually when they were teenagers around sixteen years of age. Until the day of their wedding, the boy and the girl might never have spoken to one another.

Sounds scary to modern ears, doesn't it? And yet somehow, these were mostly happy, successful marriages. Of course, not every couple had a satisfying relationship, but *most* of them did. This seems like an astounding achievement. How was it possible for people so young, naive, and unaware of the nature of the opposite sex to create happy marriages? Critics sometimes try to make the point that the young couple "didn't know any better, so they were happy with what they had." As if that's a bad thing. As if it would be better if we could tell them, "Hey, this marriage you're so satisfied with—you could do a lot better." Besides the fact that such criticism is rather perverse, it also sells short the participants, casting them as unenlightened dupes.

The reason these marriages worked so often and so well is that both husband and wife had a healthy respect for marriage. Contrary to popular opinion, marriage is not "what you make it." What an awful expression! The implication is that marriage will be only what the two of you create, suggesting that the marriage is solely dependent on the feelings one has about the other and that the success of the entire marriage depends somehow on the right measure of emotion and care you put into it.

While it is indubitably so that we must invest our marriages with love and compassion and respect and care, there is much more to the marriage than our meager contribution. When you think that you "made" the marriage, then you are lifting a great burden onto your own shoulders and it isn't long before you discover what an overwhelming task you've given yourself.

We need to think about this in another way. The act of marriage transforms the individuals involved; a holy bond now exists between husband and wife, granting their life together with a new dimension that is beyond their individual contributions. In other words, marriage is something sacred long before two people get married. Their wedding allows them to participate in this sacred dimension. When a couple is imbued with an awareness of this, the very awareness empowers and transforms the relationship. You are part of something that is so much more than what the two of you can possibly contribute.

Appreciating the awesomeness of marriage actually helps two people stay married. That's because any possible stresses along the way are not about just him or just her anymore. It's all about the marriage, which itself is holy and special. Problems become solvable because both are working on a goal that is greater than the individual self. When you value marriage it takes far less effort to make it work, because you understand its inherent value. Yes, we must put effort into our marriages, but we are supported by an amazing power inherent in marriage. Focusing on the awesome power of marriage and viewing the role of husband or wife as a sacred responsibility, enables a person to make a happy marriage.

If you are blessed, your marriage will last a very long time. Over the course of a lifetime, every person changes. Both you and your spouse will change. Throughout all these alterations and transitions, one's attitude toward marriage can remain fixed and constant and that will make all the difference through the years. During the dating period, before you get married, you can do yourself a favor by finding out what the other person's attitude toward marriage is, rather than just his attitude toward you. Does he believe in marriage? Is he in awe of it? If not, then why is he getting married?

Ask *yourself* the following: Are *you* in awe of marriage? Do you believe that you should get married, regardless of whether or not you are in the mood to get married? Do you believe you are supposed to be married, because that is the only right way to be? If not, then don't get married. Don't make a lifelong commitment to something that you don't believe in—with anybody.

CHAPTER SEVEN

What Is "Good Chemistry"?

Well-known is the advice that a person needs to have good chemistry with the one he marries. It's not enough to know intellectually that this person is a good person, likely to be a good provider, does mitzvos, etc. One's heart also needs to feel a pull toward the other person. The question is, what constitutes good chemistry? It's not so easy to define exactly what this means.

A good gauge for judging chemistry is to take a good look at the sort of awareness generated by being in the company of the other. Suppose a man is sitting with a woman and he suddenly becomes very aware of himself. He wonders if he's actually behaving enough like a man. All sorts of thoughts may begin to arise: *Maybe she doesn't respect me. Maybe I'm not making the right impression. Maybe I should act a little more tough. Maybe I should be a little more gentle.* All these thoughts and doubts race through his mind, leaving him uncomfortable with himself. What is he so uncomfortable about? The self-awareness that the energy between him and this particular woman has generated has made him uncomfortable.

This sort of discomfort only happens when he is around certain women. Around other women, he may feel very comfortable and at ease. If he sits on one side of a table and a woman sits on the other, and he feels comfortable with who he is, that's called good chemistry. That is a drawing of his heart toward hers. He is free from self-examination to be able to exchange ideas and thoughts with her. That's pretty good.

"Excitement" is not what we're talking about. Excitement, especially right at the outset, is different; if sitting with a woman on a date makes this young man very excited about her, that's tricky. In such a case, it's harder to tell if he's really experiencing good chemistry or if there's something else distorting his clarity.

If you're comfortable with yourself when you're around a woman and you feel like a man, or you're a woman who is feeling comfortable when on a date with a man, that's a good sign.

CHAPTER EIGHT

The Key to Safe, Sane, and Constructive Dating

Traditionally, Jewish people have dated through a matchmaker, popularly known as a shadchan. In this generation, many frustrated singles argue that the traditional "shidduch system" style of dating no longer works. This couldn't be further from the truth. The shidduch system is perfect. Considering all the complaints raised against it, it is still the best system possible. Many of the problems people encounter in shidduchim could be remedied with a change in perspective.

The key to smart dating is not allowing yourself to get invested emotionally before you get engaged. Don't make yourself vulnerable only to find out that he or she will not marry you. Don't ever get attached to somebody who is not yours. You go out on the date, you meet the person, and you go home. That's all you have to do.

I know what you're thinking: *It's not that simple.* But despite all the problems that come up in the shidduch system, using a shadchan will save you a lot of pain, frustration, and drama. A shadchan keeps things cool and level-headed. You and the person you're dating do not call each other. You let the shadchan communicate on your behalf and you allow the shadchan to plan the dates. You and your date are not best friends. You don't owe each other anything. Until you are married, you need to do whatever you can to keep yourself from getting emotionally attached.

Stay neutral—and not only neutral, but selfish. Don't think you have to go out with someone again or propose to them simply because you don't want to hurt their feelings. That's acting as if you're already married to the person. For now, be selfish. You'll have plenty of time to be selfless once you're married.

If you're bored, turned off, or uninterested, then walk away. It's that simple. Don't drag it out. Granted, this might not sound nice. However, the one to whom you should be nice is your husband or your wife. Don't waste time being nice to someone you're currently dating. Some people are so nice to their dates and terrible to their spouses—they have their priorities backward.

When you see bad traits that you cannot tolerate in your date, end it. Some say, "I'm dating a guy with very bad habits,

THE KEY TO SAFE, SANE, AND CONSTRUCTIVE DATING

but I see potential in him." Save that kind of talk for your husband. A date has no potential. Either it's good or it's over. Notice I said to be selfish. That doesn't mean you should be cruel or nasty. You need to look out for your own interests. You're not going out on a date to do anyone a favor. You're on the date to see if the other person is right for you. You're checking them out.

Once you're married and you finally see the flaws in your spouse, that's the time to be nice. That's the time to just smile and say that he or she has potential.

For now, be selfish.
You'll have plenty of time to be
selfless once you're married.

CHAPTER NINE

Toxic Idea: Maybe I'll Never Get Married

Some people, in their discouragement at how long it's taking to find their bashert, begin to think they will never get married. Banish that thought from your head right now! Rest assured that the other half of your soul is out there. G-d originally created Adam and Chava as one body. Their subsequent separation was only for the purpose of their eventual reunification. So too, everyone has their other half waiting for them. G-d will surely bring you together. It is G-d's will that it should happen, and so it will happen. In the meantime, stay focused.

For now, it helps not to think about the idea that you have to marry a man or marry a woman. Instead, focus on finding your husband or your wife. The verse in the Torah says, "A man leaves his parents and cleaves to his wife" (Genesis 2:24)—he does not cleave to a *woman*. This is why women should not be thinking about men and men should not be thinking about women. Think of it this way: your job is only to look for your spouse.

We need to think rationally. Rational thinking means: *I'm probably typical. If the vast majority of people find a spouse, then I will, too.* If you allow yourself to think that you might not get married because there are some people who don't and you may be one of them, then you are looking at yourself as an exception rather than as typical.

Don't pay attention to statistics and don't entertain scary thoughts about never getting married. Try to tackle the short-term frustrations in a more businesslike manner. A shadchan didn't call you back? Then call a different shadchan. As we have said, your marriage is not up to them. Only G-d can determine whom you marry and when it happens. The only variable is the channel through which your bashert will arrive. He or she might come through Shadchan A or Shadchan B, or not through a shadchan at all! G-d has many emissaries, but always keep in the forefront of your mind that it is only G-d who calls the shots.

Trust in G-d and stay focused on your individual mission.

CHAPTER TEN

Shidduch Crisis: Myth or Fact?

I often hear single people not only complain about being single, but also about the fact that many of their friends can't seem to get married as well. They feel that if this is the case, there must be a crisis!

Some years ago, within a very short period of time, a series of tragedies befell the Montreal Jewish community. Numerous people wrote letters to the Lubavitcher Rebbe proclaiming that everything was going wrong. There seemed to be one misfortune after another.

The Rebbe was asked what could potentially be the cause of this phenomenon. The Rebbe replied that goodness, kedusha (holiness), works in groups and through cooperation. But kelipa—the opposite of holiness—does not operate via teamwork. Bad, the Rebbe said, never collaborates with bad.

The story is relevant to our question about the supposed shidduch crisis. The Rebbe taught a lesson here, that bad things are incapable of working cooperatively with one another. Therefore, if we come up against a series of unfortunate events, we must steer clear of classifying them as part of one unified negative whole. If three bad things happen, they are three independent, separate, unrelated events. One is not connected to the other. There is no "conspiracy" at work.

Is there a "shidduch crisis"? The entire question is counterproductive. What would a shidduch crisis have to do with you? It's not as if a group of single women got together and decided, "Let's create a crisis." The fact that there are other people who are still unmarried has nothing to do with you. Isn't it remarkable just how quickly the crisis vanishes once you get engaged?

Don't consider yourself part of a crisis, and don't subscribe to "group thinking." You don't get married as a group, just as you don't stay single as a group. Getting married is not a group project. It's time for you to stop thinking in crisis terms and to start thinking as an individual. Finding your bashert is a private matter that is between only you, your future husband, and G-d.

CHAPTER ELEVEN

Does the Shadchan System Still Work?

In recent years, many have voiced dissatisfaction with the method of using a shadchan, the traditional method of dating that has been the primary way Jews have searched for a marriage partner since biblical times. I'm often asked if this approach still works. Recently someone wrote to me, "For five years I've been in touch with numerous shadchanim and I haven't received a call from a single one of them. Do you think the shadchan system needs to change?"

Others ask about Shabbat retreats and events held for a mixed crowd of men and women. They think perhaps those would be more effective. What can we do to make it easier for singles to get married? In truth, the way in which any single will find their spouse remains impossible to predict and shrouded in mystery. Sometimes it happens through a matchmaker, another time a match is made through a friend or relative, and in a third case, it seems to come about by accident. How and when it will happen, only G-d knows.

The key point to remember is that it is G-d Who arranges matches, and no one else. The matchmaker does not have any control over when or how you'll meet your spouse, and neither do your friends. All you need to do is put your best foot forward and let G-d take it from there. You don't have to figure it all out. This is the mindset you must have when searching for your better half.

Unfortunately, it's common for people to blame their prolonged state of singlehood on the matchmakers. But the matchmakers are not in charge and though they may think they can persuade the upper worlds, in fact, they do not do so. Finding your match doesn't depend on your behavior. So blaming yourself or others for your circumstances is not the answer. In fact, it's completely counterproductive. You have to believe that every single match is a miracle.

The simple fact that two halves of one soul manage to find one another in this big, crazy, mixed-up world is nothing short of miraculous. But matchmakers don't perform miracles; that is not their job. They merely do what they have to do to help the miracle become a reality.

Matches are made in Heaven; not by matchmakers. Jewish tradition teaches us that the one you are supposed to marry is the one you will marry. No shadchan—no matter how bad—can stop that from happening. You are not dependent on a matchmaker for finding your shidduch; you call them only because you are supposed to make an effort in this matter.

Furthermore, it's not as if a shadchan knows the secret to matching people up, for very often we see matches that seem to make little sense. That's because shidduchim are miracles, and marriage is not something that "makes sense." Matchmakers employ their own logic and reason to figure out which matches to try to arrange. In reality, there is no discernible rhyme or reason to explain why two people end up together. People marry exactly whom they are supposed to marry simply because G-d arranges events so that predestined matches take place.

Even after we get married, we might fail to appreciate that it is G-d who makes matches. Sometimes we may feel that we have found the perfect match, and at other times we may feel that we married the wrong one. We may think that perhaps we made a mistake! This is nonsense. The one we're supposed to be with is not determined by what we think or how we feel. G-d knows exactly what He is doing. So let go and trust Him.

The key point to remember
is that it is G-d Who arranges
matches, and no one else.

CHAPTER TWELVE

The Art of Optimism

Here's a true story. A matchmaker suggested a certain young man for a certain young lady (let's call her Chaya). Chaya refused to go out with the fellow because, although he was only in his twenties, he was already starting to lose his hair. Several weeks later, the matchmaker thought of another match (let's call him Mendel). Mendel and Chaya seemed like they would make a lovely couple. There was only one problem: Mendel was completely bald! After speaking to the young man on the phone, the matchmaker suggested he wear a hat throughout the entire date.

"Whatever you do," she advised, "don't take off your hat."

After the date, the matchmaker called Mendel. "Nu?" she asked. "How did it go?"

"It went very well!" replied Mendel enthusiastically. "We had a nice time. Oh, but I forgot what you said and halfway through the date, I took my hat off."

The matchmaker's heart sank. She called Chaya, sure that it was all over between Chaya and Mendel. "Well, how did it go?" the matchmaker asked apprehensively.

"Great," said Chaya.

"Really?" the matchmaker exclaimed, unable to contain her surprise. "It was good?"

"Yes," she responded.

"So, you'll go out with him again?"

"Yes!" Chaya exclaimed.

"Even though he's bald?"

An astonished Chaya answered, "He's bald?!"

When it's bashert, you don't notice any faults; when it's not, you won't notice any virtues.

A lot of people worry about glitches in their résumés. They worry that they're bald, they worry that they're too tall, they worry that they have acne, that they weigh too much, that they are shy. The first rule of dating has to be *Don't worry*.

To worry is to demonstrate a lack of trust in G-d. It's also a complete waste of time.

Let G-d do the worrying. The Talmud teaches that G-d spends most of His nights making matches. He sees to it that every person has a partner and makes sure everyone ultimately finds their match. Whether one finds their match today or tomorrow, it will happen at the right time, so it does no good to worry. It doesn't matter what your level of intelligence is, whether or not you have money, or what family you come from. Every situation is different, but every match ultimately gets made. Therefore, there is no such thing as a "difficult match." The idea that it is harder for some people to get married than it is for others is false, because *every* match is difficult. In fact, the Talmud likens finding a spouse to parting the Red Sea! From our limited vantage point, some matches appear especially difficult to make while others may seem easy, but to G-d it's all the same.

But should I really be optimistic? If you have been looking for someone to marry for a very long time, dating for years and years with no success, you might be wondering why you shouldn't worry. The simple answer is yes, you should be optimistic! G-d wants you to be married much more than you yourself want to be married. Reread that last sentence whenever you start to have doubts.

G-d wants you to be married even more than you want to be married. Why? Because it was *His* idea that you should get married in the first place. It's G-d who invented the idea of marriage. He's the one who wants people to get married, He decides who will marry whom, and He arranges the matches. From choosing the match to making sure the couple gets to the chuppah, G-d does it all. And if G-d wants something, what's to stop Him? So, yes, you can and you *should* be confident and optimistic. Every match that needs to be made will be made in the best way and at the best time.

CHAPTER THIRTEEN

What Will My Friends Think?

Time after time I've run into people who are having trouble deciding whether or not to marry the one they are dating. Occasionally, some of them are honest enough to tell me that part of their concern is "What will my friends think if I marry this person?"

The problem with that is, as mentioned, too many people are fixated on marrying *a man or a woman* rather than their husband or wife. If you believe you are simply marrying a man or a woman, then it's only natural that you'll start making comparisons. You'll notice that one girl is better looking or smarter than another. One man is richer or more capable than another. You'll always find others who have what your potential spouse lacks. If your friend's shidduch seems to have what your shidduch is missing, you'll feel resentful and ashamed.

But instead of comparison shopping for a man or a woman, think about finding your spouse. If you truly believe that everyone is married to their bashert—the husband or wife whom they were destined to marry, then what use is there for comparisons? The very concept that "Maybe I should have married his wife," or "Maybe I should have married her husband," is ridiculous, because you married the one whom G-d decided you would marry, and therefore that person is the best person *for you*.

The idea of trying to find the "best" man or woman to marry is very problematic and not a Jewish approach to marriage. It causes trouble for those who are trying to get married and it can prevent people from staying married. It's simply not correct "marriage thinking." You need to ask yourself the following: "Do I want to be married, or do I want to find somebody?" Make up your mind. These two options are not the same at all. The common and wrong approach is "I want to go out and meet someone and if everything fits, we'll get married." No. The priority attitude in getting married is not that "everything fits" but that you are focused on marriage itself and on finding the one with whom you are meant to build a life. Of course, you will want to like the person you marry, have compatible values, and find them reasonably attractive. But the primary reason you get married is because marriage itself is good and you believe that marriage has inherent value.

If someone says, "I don't want to get married, but I met someone special so I'm going to marry him or her," I can promise you there will be trouble down the line. It is a bad idea to marry someone only because you may think the person is wonderful and magnificent right now. That's because nobody is so wonderful and so magnificent that you can live with them for more than a week. When you spend that much time with someone, there's no way you're going to enjoy every minute of it. Such a marriage is headed for a crisis because you never wanted to get married in the first place. You wanted to be with someone magnificent, and there is no one on earth who is pleasant to be around all the time. It's not even fair for the recipient. If you marry me only because I'm magnificent, that's not fair to me, because I cannot be magnificent every day. I'm a human being and I'll be better company some days than others.

Marriage itself has to be the purpose, the objective, and the ideal. Let's restore marriage to its central place of importance. Marriage should be considered of more importance than questions of whom we're going to marry. It will make things a lot less confusing. When you approach marriage with this mindset, you have no worries about what your friends will think.

The primary reason you
get married is because marriage
itself is good and you believe that
marriage has inherent value.

CHAPTER FOURTEEN

Am I Being Too Picky?

Young men and women go on one or more dates, and then they complain about all the many things that are wrong with the person they dated. In one case the issue is a lack of physical attraction. Other times the person shows a lack of spirituality, or is not chassidish (pious) enough, or is too chassidish. Then there are times when it's not a fit emotionally.

In your dating, is there always something wrong? If so, you have to start suspecting that something is fundamentally wrong with your approach. Is every possible shidduch impossible?

A person is always looking for the perfect spouse—and why not? A great person deserves the perfect spouse. However, singles often have in mind an image of something that doesn't exist. He doesn't want to marry a wife—he wants to marry a "perfect." If he or she is generally uncomfortable with the people they date, this implies that perhaps they only like perfection.

If we straighten out our views in this area, it would greatly help us to marry correctly. Get it right, and the right person will come along.

CHAPTER FIFTEEN

How to Prevent Dating Suicide

The worst thing you can do after the date is to come home and torture yourself by wondering whether you could spend the rest of your life with this person. After the first date, focus only on whether you could spend another hour with her. After the second date, ask yourself if you can tolerate another hour; after the third date, another hour; and so on.

We have a very good system, yet unfortunately people aren't using it to full advantage because they don't appreciate its tremendous value. It's become a mishugas (craziness) that after the first date the singles stop talking to the shadchan and begin speaking to each other directly. There should be a law against it. It's terrible.

It's inhumane because when you eliminate the shadchan, there's no nice way to call off the shidduch. Even worse, he goes out with her again and tells her in person why she's not right for him. What a horrible thing it is to hurt another person's feelings this way! I have heard the same story from a number of girls about why they have stopped going out altogether—because a guy told her why he doesn't want her.

As bad as the shadchan is (no one says they are all good), they serve an absolutely vital purpose. And they need to be used to the very end of the dating process, until you get engaged. When you have a shadchan, your shadchan will straighten out any misunderstandings that might have taken place on a date. The shadchan will get answers to questions you would be (and should be) uncomfortable asking the person directly. And very importantly, the shadchan will find out if the other party is ready for marriage or not and can accurately advise you. A girl can ruin things by telling a guy she's ready before he is. Then he is left unsure about what to do, and the shidduch can be completely derailed. Or the guy can wreck things by proposing on the second or third date and scaring the girl out of her wits. So in fact, in cases like these, skipping the shadchan is next to suicide.

Respect for the privacy of the person you are dating is extremely important. Another nasty thing: a guy goes out, decides not to marry the girl, and then describes her to all his friends in detail. Is this not criminal? We've lost our decency when speaking about such private matters.

Here's a true story (names changed) about what great things can happen when people are discreet and the shadchan is used correctly.

Rachel went out with David a few times. He was nice and fine in every way, except there was no chemistry. Rachel also felt he wasn't very sensitive. She told the shadchan her feelings, but no one else, and the shidduch ended. A few months later, David got engaged to Rachel's classmate Sarah. When wishing her friend mazel tov, Rachel played dumb and asked Sarah, "What stands out about David?" Sarah said excitedly, "Ohhh, David is so *sensitive*!" Nearly forty years later, David is, thank G-d, still sharing his sensitivity with Sarah.

Whether they're good or not, whether you like them or not, the shadchan is a gift—a buffer to protect feelings and maintain dignity at what can be a vulnerable time in singles' lives. Accept the shadchan gratefully and use him or her to the fullest.

The shadchan is a gift—
a buffer to protect feelings and
maintain dignity at what can be a
vulnerable time in singles' lives.

CHAPTER SIXTEEN

The Golden Rule in Dating

A woman asks, "Where are all the men? I'm trying to get married!"

"All the men? Are you going to marry all the men?"

"No, I'm trying to find a special man."

"You have found many special men. They happened to be married or are not interested in you, but they are special."

"Okay, I'm looking for the one for me."

"You mean *your* husband? Now you're making sense."

Looking for *your* husband is a long way from wondering where "all the men" are. Since you are not looking for "a man" but for your husband, what is the essential difference between the two? The problem is that if you have not got a definition of a husband, then how are you going to be a wife?

Are you looking for a man to marry? Don't! We already know that men are from Mars and women from Venus, and therefore they don't get along very well. Men are known to have opinions. Any man you marry will have his own set of wants and needs. He'll have his own plans, his own shtick—whims, oddities, maybe even eccentricities. And you know about yourself that you already have your own opinions, your own wants and needs, your own shtick. See the problem? You're asking for trouble if you marry a man.

In order for a marriage to work, you need to stop trying to find a man and look for a husband instead. And you need to be a wife, not a woman. There is a profound difference.

Today, we're inundated from the outside world with unhealthy messages and images about relationships between men and women. Even the most pious of Jews, who believe they have insulated themselves, can fall prey to foreign points of view. This barrage of persuasive imagery has created the wish, in most of us, to meet a man or a woman whom we like and then we will live together forevermore. But he will not become a husband and she will not become a wife because husbands and wives are not glamorous enough. Wives are always "desperate," while girls can enjoy a night out. Husbands are "demanding," while guys are exciting.

The truth is that men and women are healthier without each other, for they usually act in their own interest, often to the detriment of the other. But a husband and wife? A husband and a wife cannot exist without each other. In a real marriage, he ceases to be a mere "man" and she is no longer just a "woman." They are participants in a marriage, a grand and awesome project in which former habits, say flirting with the opposite sex, are not only inappropriate, they are irrelevant. It would be like having been already elected president of the United States and then running for mayor of Skunktown, Nevada. Why would you do that? It used to be that people valued and honored marriage, embracing its responsibilities with a sense of awe. It is time to look away from ideas that undermine and destroy marriage and refocus on the beauty of the union of a husband and a wife.

A husband and a wife cannot exist
without each other. In a real marriage,
he ceases to be a mere "man" and
she is no longer just a "woman."

CHAPTER SEVENTEEN

Is This It? How to Know If She's the One

Over the years, many singles have told me they go on dates with many different people but none of the people they've dated seem to be "the one." The question that plagues them is this: "When the 'right one' comes along, how will I know?"

The truth is, you *can't* tell who your predestined soulmate is. Such matters are hidden to all but G-d. And you don't have to know if he or she is the one. What you need to know before you propose is that you have met somebody who you hope is the one. If you have a strong desire in your heart that you would really, really like her to be the one, then that's all you need. The rest is up to G-d. If she is the one, then you will marry her. If she is not the one, then you won't end up married to her even though you think she *should* be the one.

What do you need to know when you're deciding to marry? You need to know that you have homshochas halev—a drawing of the heart—toward her. You need to have the feeling that you would like her to be the one whom you would bring into *your* life so that together, the two of you will build a successful life.

In Mishneh Torah, a book of Jewish law, the great scholar Maimonides writes that a man must have his own home before getting married. This is an incredibly important point. Maimonides didn't mean a home in the literal sense. What he meant was something on a deeper level, akin to the modern saying, "Get your house in order." *Before you get married you really need to have a life.* When you get married, you bring your spouse into your world. But before you can do that, you need to have a world, a life! Otherwise, after you get married, where are you taking her?

CHAPTER EIGHTEEN

The Secret to Praying for Your Shidduch

Many women have complained to me, "I don't know why G-d doesn't answer me! I keep praying and pleading and crying to meet a guy, but nothing comes of it." If this is the prayer, is it really possible G-d hasn't answered it? Is it really possible that the woman asking this question has never met a guy?

It is true that G-d knows what is hidden in our hearts, even that which we cannot speak. Nonetheless, *we* should be a little more conscious of what it is we are asking for and the way we speak to G-d. It's important *we* know what we are asking for.

When you pray to find a shidduch, you need to be specific. Don't simply ask to meet a "man" or a "woman." Ask G-d to introduce you to your husband or your wife. And don't just ask to meet your spouse. What good is it to only meet someone? You want to be married to your spouse—and not only married, but settled with a family. That's how you should pray when seeking a shidduch.

I'm reminded of the following story. A man came to his rabbi and complained that he didn't have enough money.

"You have to trust in G-d!" urged his rabbi.

"I keep praying and asking G-d!" the man protested.

"What exactly do you ask for?" the rabbi asked.

"I ask G-d to find me a job!" replied the man.

The man in the story didn't want a job. He wanted to be rich! If he had only just said so, perhaps G-d would have granted his prayer. We need to work on being honest with G-d. When you pray, just be straight with Him. Don't be afraid to be blunt. Tell Him the truth. Don't ask to meet a man, not even a certain kind of man—ask to get married to your husband. You're not a character in a romance novel. You are a Jew who wants to build a home and a life with the other half of your soul. So stop wasting your time. Cut to the chase and ask G-d to give you exactly what you need. Ask Him to get you married to your spouse.

CHAPTER NINETEEN

Fast Track to Your Bashert?

I don't know if you can speed up the process of finding your bashert, but you can certainly make the search feel less torturous. It doesn't have to be a difficult, painful, drawn-out ordeal. The bottom line is this: If you trust in G-d, remain focused on the important things, don't get caught up in the less important details, and give yourself time to become the best husband or wife you can be, you're on the right track. If you've been paying attention to what I've been saying until now, you know that it is a far better use of your time to prepare yourself to be a proper spouse than it is to worry about whom you're going to marry.

Work on becoming the right person, and eventually you'll find the right person. Marriage means *I have a life that is precious, a life that is worth sharing with someone else.* The richer your life is, the richer your marriage will be. So, enrich your life. That's the most important thing to do while you're single. Everything else will fall into place.

Make an effort. We all know that finding our soulmate is a blessing from Above and that everyone finds their soulmate at the right time. But in order to receive any blessing from G-d, we have to put forth our own efforts. *Study all the teachings from the Rebbe.* Have trust in G-d and focus on the things you need to concentrate on now. Give yourself time to get ready to be a good husband or a good wife, to create a good home. Then you will be ready and confident for marriage.

In the secular world, marriages often fail because people mistakenly think they will build a life with the one they marry, rather than working on having their own lives first. We often see amazing (and tired) parents who spend their entire day schlepping the kids around, taking them to karate, soccer practice, ballet, and helping them with their homework. Those parents live entirely for their children, but they don't get to have a life of their own.

Living for your children is not the way to do things. Parents are supposed to have their own lives and children are supposed to build their existence around the parents' lives. Not the other way around. Of course, children need loving and tuned-in parents, but it is much healthier for kids to model themselves on the example of parents who are engaged in important worthwhile pursuits. The parents' value system is transmitted to the children through the way they live.

The same turnaround needs to be applied here. Instead of worrying about what you can do to hurry the process of meeting your soulmate, use your time to enrich the present moment to develop what you will share with your future spouse and transmit to your children, G-d willing. But don't get too obsessive about it. Read *Sichos,* the Rebbe's talks, and try your absolute best. G-d wants you married. He's working on it full-time. If you don't know how to make a keli, a vessel, G-d will make one for you. He doesn't abandon anyone because of their inabilities.

Remember to relax, both now and after you get married. When you are married, make sure to express to your children the phenomenal gift that marriage is. You want them to appreciate the holiness and awesomeness of it. Make sure they are generous, patient, and respectful enough so that they can make their own marriages the best they can be. The rest is commentary.

Remember that for G-d, there never is a crisis. Give Him a break. Let Him do His job, and we all await your good news.

If you really want to understand your spouse better, don't ask "why." Ask "what."

CHAPTER TWENTY

Bonus: The Three-Word Marriage Guidebook

The most important three words in any book on marriage are *never ask "why?"* If people would follow that advice carefully we wouldn't have to write anything else. But let us explain.

"Why" is very offensive. This one word can destroy everything you strive to create in your marriage. The "W-word" can even shatter marriages founded with the best of intentions. When your spouse expresses her needs, wants, fears, likes, dislikes, and so forth, do not ask "why." Your job is to meet the needs of your spouse, with no questions asked. Asking "why" is insensitive and dismissive. Asking "why" means, "Something bothers you? I'm not impressed. Give me a reason *why* it bothers you and then maybe I'll think about not doing that anymore."

Asking "why" trivializes your spouse's feelings and opinions. Furthermore, answering the question is frustrating, because most of the time, your spouse *doesn't even know* why something bothers him or her. So, when you force a spouse to explain why, it causes great pain and frustration.

If you really want to understand your spouse better, don't ask "why." Ask "what." "What happened? What are you feeling? What's going on?" By asking "what," you are asking for more information, which stimulates constructive communication and good conversation. Asking "why" leads to a fight. If you stop asking "why" and start asking "what," you will start to see an immediate improvement in your marriage. Try it. It works.

ACKNOWLEDGMENTS

This book, as my previous ones, was a team effort and I would like to convey my gratitude to some vital members of this team.

It may be true that one should not judge a book by its cover, but it certainly helps if the cover invites the reader to look inside. Thank you to Yossi and Chaya Mushka Kanner for their cover design and interior layout and for providing a beautiful exterior to the ideas within this book.

Thank you to Chana Greenberg for once again providing her invaluable editing expertise in compiling this work and producing the best version possible of the text.

I am very grateful to Patricia Spadaro for her expert publishing coaching, astute guidance, and detailed oversight that helped make this book shine and reach its potential.

A special thank you to my son Rabbi Zalman Friedman, executive manager of It's Good to Know, for his tireless dedication to this and so many other projects.

Many of the questions addressed in the book were posed by students and audiences during my speaking engagements. I thank them for their sincere questions and our valuable conversations on these topics. If what I have written here brings greater understanding and clarity to all who will now read this book, I am deeply grateful.

Dedicated by Leah Cohen
in loving memory of Rosie and Yoel Cohen
and Norma (Rus) Yarmark, of blessed memory.
May their legacy continue to inspire us and may
our Mitzvahs continue to uplift them.

In honor of Shalom Dovber Ben Alya Shoshana
and Chaya Sara Bas Chava and their family.

In honor of Esther Pearl Cohen and dedicated in
loving memory of Yisrael Leib ben Gutel Hakohen.
With love and appreciation from their children.

Dedicated by Jessica L. Atkins and Guillermo Pulgarin
in honor of their daughters, Sarah and Channah.

Dedicated by the Feigenbaum/Pepose family
with gratitude to Rabbi Manis Friedman.

Dedicated in memory of Harav Shimon ben Eliyahu,
of blessed memory. May his merits bring his
grandchildren happily to the chuppah and to eternal joy.

In honor of the speedy and complete recovery of our
beloved daughter Chava Guta bas Henya Chasya
by the Rivkin family.

> *Our free gift for you:*
>
> Access Rabbi Friedman's dating course for free at
> www.itsgoodtoknow.org/datingbook

Learn more about
Rabbi Manis Friedman and his work

Rabbi Manis Friedman regularly speaks and teaches at events worldwide. The most popular rabbi on YouTube, he offers free online tips and resources as well as ongoing releases on a wide range of topics, including relationships, dating, marriage and family, emotional well-being, spirituality, life's challenges, and much more.

Sign up for Rabbi Friedman's free email newsletter to get exclusive content, updates, and special offers at:
www.itsgoodtoknow.org

Stay connected:
itsgoodtoknow.org
info@itsgoodtoknow.org
facebook.com/manisfriedman
youtube.com/manisfriedman
twitter.com/manisfriedman
instagram.com/rabbimanisfriedman

RABBI MANIS FRIEDMAN is a world-renowned author, teacher, and speaker, well known for his provocative and incisive wit and wisdom. His international speaking tours, seminars, and retreats take him around the world, and he has been featured on CNN, A&E Reviews, PBS, and BBC Worldwide as well as in such publications as *The New York Times, Rolling Stone, Seventeen, Guideposts,* and *Publishers Weekly.* He is the author of *The Joy of Intimacy: A Soulful Guide to Keeping the Spark Alive; Creating a Life That Matters: How to Live and Love with Meaning and Purpose;* and *Doesn't Anyone Blush Anymore?* Rabbi Friedman is the most popular rabbi on YouTube. He is the dean of Bais Chana Institute of Jewish Studies, which he cofounded in 1971, and the founder of It's Good to Know, a nonprofit life-learning foundation based in New York City. He lives with his family in St. Paul, Minnesota. To learn more about Rabbi Manis Friedman and his work, visit ItsGoodToKnow.org.

www.ingramcontent.com/pod-product-compliance
Lightning Source LLC
Chambersburg PA
CBHW020322090426
42735CB00009B/1368